Brave Spies

Contents

Written by Sufiya Ahmed

Illustrated by Maxine Hammen

Collins

1 Special Operations Executive

In 1939, the Second World War began when **Nazi Germany** invaded Poland. Britain and France responded by declaring war on Germany.

In 1940, France was defeated and occupied by Germany. Adolf Hitler, the Nazi leader, now planned to invade Britain by air and sea.

As part of the fight back, the Prime Minister of Britain, Winston Churchill, set up a top-secret organisation called the Special Operations Executive (SOE).

Its aim was to:

- spy on the Nazis and collect information about the number of Nazi soldiers at different locations
- make it harder for the Nazis to rule the countries they had conquered, by cutting telephone lines, moving railway tracks and blowing up Nazi trucks loaded with weapons. This was known as **sabotage**.

The F Section of the SOE was for spy work related to France. It sent 470 agents to France during the Second World War, but only 39 of them were women.

The SOE recruited women because they made excellent spies. They blended into their surroundings with everyday chores, such as shopping.

The SOE F Section allowed women to join in 1942.

Winston Churchill

The F Section spies needed to be fluent French speakers. The purpose of a spy was to blend into their surroundings without arousing suspicion.

French speakers were invited to an interview at the SOE. If they agreed to accept a position, the details of the mission were explained.

The dangers, including the possibility of death if captured, were made clear.

New spies had to sign the Official Secrets Act, promising never to reveal government secrets to anyone.

Some of the women already served in the war effort by working for the Women's **Auxiliary** Air Force (WAAF) which was set up to support the Royal Air Force. Members learnt to send and receive secret messages using code. They provided weather reports to pilots, maintained aircraft and served on airfields to help the pilots fly their planes.

a young WAAF recruit

Other women who hadn't served in the WAAF were recruited for their fluent French.

Due to the urgent need to replace agents who were already caught or killed by the Nazis, the training only lasted between four and nine months.

There were 60 training schools in Britain.

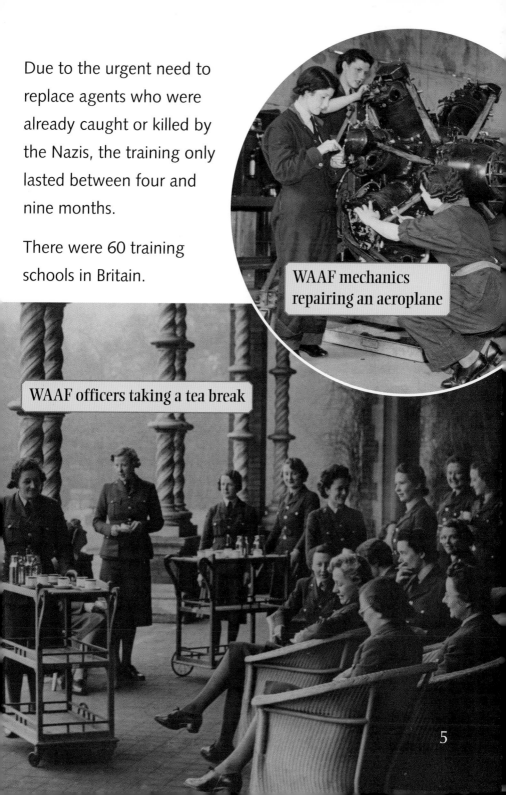

WAAF mechanics repairing an aeroplane

WAAF officers taking a tea break

Physical training for agents included cross-country running, basic weapon handling and unarmed combat.

The spies learnt how to:

- make and use explosives
- blow up bridges
- operate German, British and American weapons
- follow someone and avoid being followed
- wire railway tracks to derail trains
- parachute out of planes.

a woman training to parachute jump

2 Codenames and networks

All spies were given codenames. Their true identities remained secret. All were assigned to **networks**, which were secretly named and made up of three roles:

- Network leader: planned all the missions
- Radio operator: communicated messages to London headquarters and received instructions. This was dangerous work as the operator had to carry a radio set contained in a large suitcase. Being caught with one meant instant arrest. Most radio operators only lasted six weeks before they were captured by the Nazis.
- **Courier**: acted as the middle person between the leader and the **resistance fighters** working with the network. Their job was to pass on secret messages to the radio operator who was responsible for transmitting the messages to London.

The maquis were the French fighters who rebelled against the Nazi occupation of their country. They tried to fight back and helped the SOE spies with their missions.

The messages were sent by the radio set using Morse code.

Morse code was a way of communicating during the war using a radio set. Dots and dashes represented the alphabet letters and numbers when written down. These translated to sounds that were sent on the radio – short beeps for dots and longer beeps for dashes. A radio operator receiving a message would write down the dots and dashes and then translate the message into English.

Have a go at cracking this code!

Turn to page 10 for the Morse code symbols.

..--- -. . . .-- .- --. . . -. - ... .-- .. .-.. .-.. -.. .-. --- .--.

.. -. ..... -. .. --. ..... - ...

The Morse code symbols

A .–	M – –	Y – .– –
B – ...	N – .	Z – – ..
C – .– .	O – – –	1 .– – – –
D – ..	P .– – .	2 ..– – –
E .	Q – – .–	3 ...– –
F ..– .	R .– .	4 ....–
G – – .	S ...	5 .....
H	T –	6 – ....
I ..	U ..–	7 – – ...
J .– – –	V ...–	8 – – – ..
K – .–	W .– –	9 – – – – .
L .– ..	X – ..–	0 – – – – –

2 new agents will drop in 5 nights

The highest bravery medals were awarded after the war by Britain and France.

French military medal, Croix de Guerre, awarded for acts of heroism

George Cross, Britain's highest **civilian** award for **gallantry**

"for acts of the greatest heroism or of the most conspicuous courage in circumstances of extreme danger"

King George VI

King George VI and the future Queen Elizabeth II

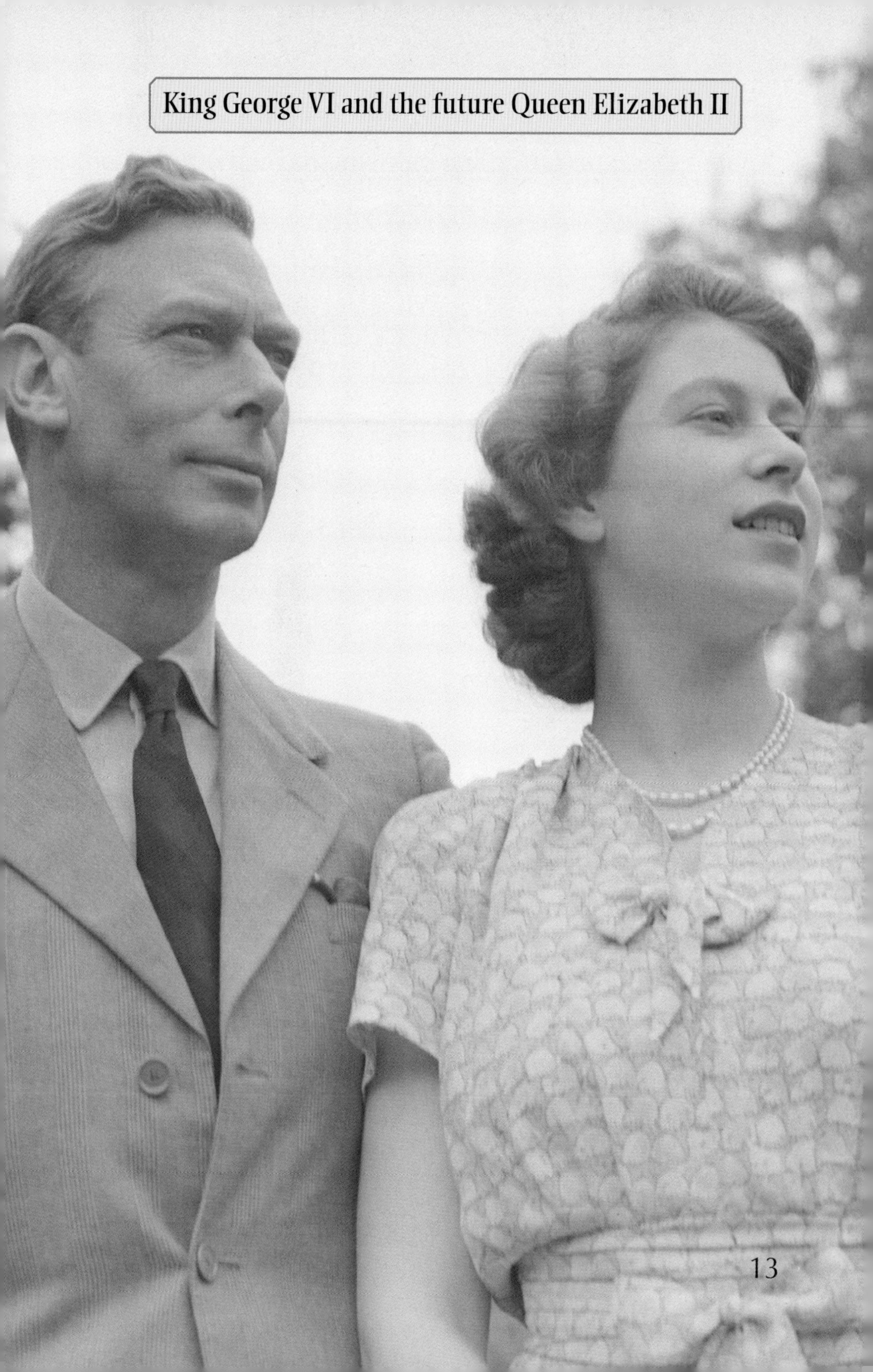

The Bravest Women of the F Section

Thirty-nine women agents were sent to France in the Second World War by the SOE.

Every single one of these women was brave and daring. Each showed courage in the face of danger when their skills were needed to help win the war. As spies, they collected and provided information about the Nazi **troops** which made all the difference when Churchill planned his counter invasion of France with his allies.

Read about the ten women who have been selected as the Bravest Women of the SOE.

3 Behind enemy lines

Andrée Borrel

Born: 18th November 1919, France

Codename: Monique/Denise

Network name: Physician

King's Commendation for Brave Conduct (*Britain*)

Croix de Guerre (*France*)

Médaille de la Résistance (*France*)

Andrée was born and raised in France. As soon as the Second World War broke out, Andrée volunteered at the French **Red Cross** to train as a nurse. She worked at a hospital until it was closed by the Nazis.

She then joined a secret group, helping people to escape Nazi-occupied France. These included British agents, Jewish people and others, who were in danger of being captured by the Nazis.

When the group's existence became known to the Nazis, it was abandoned, and the volunteers had to flee for fear of being arrested. Andrée escaped through the Pyrenees mountains to Spain and then to Portugal, and finally flew to England. Andrée was recruited to the SOE on 15th May 1942.

On 24th September 1942, Andrée was one of two female SOE agents to parachute into occupied France. The other was Lise de Baissac. They were meant to land in France the night before, but the pilot could not locate the field lights on the ground – the sign that it was safe for the agents to parachute down.

The pilot, Andrée and Lise flew back to France the following night. This time, lights were flashed by the agents on the ground and Andrée became the first SOE female spy to land behind enemy lines.

Andrée was part of an operation called "Whitebeam". Her job was to help set up local maquis – French resistance groups – where she trained civilian men to use weapons.

As a French woman, Andrée had in-depth knowledge of her country. She helped organise parachute drops of weapons and supplies to aid the resistance.

What happened to Andrée?

The Physician network became too large and successful in its missions. Nazi officers noticed and vowed to catch the SOE spies. On 23rd June 1943, Andrée was arrested with other network members, and transferred to a **concentration camp**. She did not survive the war.

4 The torch carrier

Cecily Lefort

Born: 30th April 1899,
London

Codename: Alice

Network name: Jockey

Croix de Guerre
(*France*)

Member of the Order
of the British Empire
(*Britain*)

Cecily Lefort was of Irish **descent** and married a French
doctor in 1925. They lived together in Paris. When France
fell in 1940, Cecily fled to England before she could be
arrested by the Nazis as a British-born person.

In June 1941, Cecily joined the WAAF to help with the war effort. In 1943, she was recruited by the SOE for her ability to speak fluent French and her knowledge of French manners and style.

Cecily flew to France on a small plane with two other agents, Noor Inayat Khan and Diana Rowden, on 16th June 1943. Cecily cycled 11 kilometres to the village of Angers and then caught a train to Montélimar in south-east France. Her job was to collect information about the Nazis which was sent to London by the radio operators.

Weeks after Cecily's arrival in Montélimar, Churchill ordered the **Allied troops** to invade Sicily. The Italians were on the side of the Germans. Montélimar was located very close to the Italian border and it therefore fell on the Jockey network to supply the weapons to the Allied soldiers.

Cecily used her time to research locations where the British planes could drop weapons and supplies without being spotted. She was responsible for guiding planes by holding up a spotlight in the middle of a field. This enabled the pilot to drop the load in the correct place rather than a Nazi base.

What happened to Cecily?

The Jockey network's success in sabotage activities was noticed by Nazi officers. Determined to close the network down, they began to hunt its members. They found out the name of the local maquis leader and sent soldiers to his house on 15th September 1943. Cecily was inside and hid in the cellar. The Nazis arrested her as soon as she was found. Cecily was sent to a concentration camp. She did not survive the war.

5 Code to London

Lilian Rolfe

Born: 26th April 1914, France

Codename: Nadine

Network name: Historian

Croix de Guerre
(*France*)

Member of the Order of the British Empire
(*Britain*)

Lilian Rolfe was the daughter of a British **accountant** who worked in Paris. In 1930, the family moved to Brazil. Her first job was at the Canadian embassy, but she moved to work at the **British embassy** as soon as the war broke out.

In 1943, she moved to England and joined the WAAF to help with the war effort. Her French fluency was noticed and she was recruited to the SOE where she trained as a radio operator.

On 5th April 1944, Lilian landed in a plane near the city of Orléans in France. She joined her fellow agents at the Historian network and became busy transmitting radio messages to London headquarters.

Lilian's information included German troop movements, and location spots for arms and supply drops. She also threw herself into helping the maquis fighters in their battles with Nazi soldiers.

What happened to Lilian?

Lilian was captured on 31st July 1944 from the house where she was transmitting radio messages to London. She was sent to a concentration camp. She did not survive the war.

6 The telephone cutter

Denise Bloch

Born: 21st January 1916,
France

Codename: Ambroise

Network name: Clergyman

King's Commendation
for Brave Conduct
(*Britain*)

Médaille de la
Résistance (*France*)

Knight of the Legion
of Honour (*France*)

Croix de Guerre
(*France*)

Denise Bloch was born to a Jewish family in Paris. Her father and two brothers were soldiers in the French army and were taken prisoner by the Nazis in 1940 when France was defeated.

Denise, her mother and a third brother managed to avoid capture by using false identity papers. At the time, all Jewish people in France were being sent away to live in camps.

The family managed to escape Paris and made their way to the city of Lyon. There, Denise was recruited to work with the resistance. Her main task was to work as a translator to an SOE agent named Brian Stonehouse. Within months of joining Brian, he was arrested.

Fearful of capture, Denise dyed her hair blonde and moved to another area where she continued to work with the resistance. It was decided by the network that Denise should be sent to London to formally train as an agent.

The journey to London was not straightforward and took her 21 days. She had to walk through the Pyrenees mountains for 17 hours to reach Spain. She finally reached London on 21st May 1943. She was given false papers to travel with by British agents at every stop.

In England, Denise was trained as a radio operator and returned to France on 2nd March 1944 on a small plane.

It was incredibly brave of Denise to return to France. Not only was she known to the Nazis as an agent because of her work with Brian Stonehouse, but she was also Jewish. By this stage in the war, all known Jewish people were being sent to concentration camps.

Denise was based in the Nantes area for
the Clergyman network. She worked both as a courier
and radio operator, and also helped to sabotage
the Nazis by cutting railway and telephone lines.

What happened to Denise?

Denise was arrested in June 1944 in a house raid by Nazi
officers with other members of her network. She was
in the kitchen preparing dinner. Denise was sent to
a concentration camp. She did not survive the war.

7 Lady leader

Pearl Witherington

Born: 24th June 1914,
Paris

Codename: Marie/Pauline

Network name: Stationer/
Wrestler

Commander of
the Order of
the British Empire
(*Britain*)

Officer of the Legion
of Honour (*France*)

Pearl Witherington and her three sisters escaped France when it fell to the Nazis. The family arrived in London in July 1941 and she immediately joined the WAAF.

Pearl joined the SOE in June 1943. She became the number-one shooter with a gun.

Her trainers said she was the "best shot" to ever walk through the SOE training schools. Pearl also had a photographic memory and was able to memorise all writing before destroying it. This meant that she was never caught with any material that could endanger her.

Pearl parachuted into France on 22nd September 1943 to work as a courier for the Stationer network. With her codename Marie, she pretended to work as a beauty saleswoman so she could travel to deliver messages for her network. She spent much of her time on trains, sleeping in many of them, and having her fake ID papers constantly checked by the French police and Nazi soldiers.

When her network leader was arrested and sent to a concentration camp, Pearl formed a new network and named it Wrestler. Her new codename was Pauline. She was the only woman to lead an SOE network and local maquis.

On 11th June 1944, the Nazis attacked her village headquarters.

Pearl grabbed the tin of money that the SOE had sent and fled to nearby wheat fields. She hid as the soldiers destroyed the weapons that the SOE had dropped. Thirty-two maquis fighters tried to fight back and were killed by the Nazis that day.

The next day, Pearl emerged from the field and cycled to a neighbouring location where she met up with a radio operator named Philippe de Vomécourt. They contacted London and only days later, on 24th June, three British planes dropped new supplies of weapons.

Pearl was back to work sabotaging the Nazis.

What happened to Pearl?

Pearl survived the war. She died in 2008 at the age of 93.

8 Hunted in Paris

Noor Inayat Khan

Born: 1st January 1914,
    Russia

Codename: Madeleine

Network name: Cinema

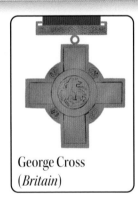

George Cross
(*Britain*)

Croix de Guerre
(*France*)

Noor-un-nissa Inayat Khan, known as Noor, was a British Indian princess, the descendent of the last ruler of Mysore in India. She was a British citizen because India was ruled by the **British Empire** at that time. She was born in Russia to an Indian father and American mother.

When Noor was a baby, the family moved to London where they remained for a few years before relocating to France.

When war broke out, Noor trained with the French Red Cross as a nurse. As soon as France fell to the Nazis, Noor fled her Paris home with her mother, sister and brother for England.

On arrival, she volunteered to work as a nurse. However, she soon itched for something more exciting to do.
Seeing an advert which invited women to join the WAAF, she applied and was recruited to train as a radio operator. Her Morse code speed was brilliant. She was soon spotted by the SOE who were searching for fluent French speakers.

On 16th June 1943, Noor was flown into the French countryside on a small plane with Cecily Lefort and Diana Bowden.

Noor made her way to Paris where she joined her new spy colleagues. Within days of arriving, her network was betrayed to the Nazis and soldiers swooped in to make arrests. Noor and a few agents fled to the French countryside to hide. Only days later, Noor decided that she would return to Paris to perform her work as a radio operator. The Nazis did not know her name because she had only just arrived. She returned to Paris and continued to send vital information to London headquarters.

The streets of Paris were always full of Nazi soldiers and officers, and it was incredibly dangerous to carry the radio set around. She hid the set in big shopping baskets and in a baby pram that she pushed around. Noor disguised herself by frequently dying her hair colour from black to brown to red.

What happened to Noor?

Noor was arrested by Nazi officers at her flat on 13th October 1943. Someone had betrayed her. She was transferred to a prison camp and did not survive the war.

9 The White Mouse

Nancy Wake

Born: 30th August 1912,
New Zealand

Codename: Hélène

Network name:
She was not part of a network

Companion of the
Order of Australia

George Medal
(*Britain*)

Knight of the Legion
of Honour (*France*)

Croix de Guerre
(*France*)

Médaille de la
Résistance (*France*)

Medal for Freedom
(*United States*)

RSA Badge in Gold
(*New Zealand*)

Born in New Zealand, Nancy Wake's family moved to Paris in the 1930s where she married a Frenchman named Henri. When war broke out, Nancy helped people flee France by escaping through Spain. Nancy's resistance activities became known to the Nazis so she fled to London in 1943. Her husband Henri was captured and executed.

The SOE immediately recruited her and she returned to France by parachuting into the countryside on 30th April 1944. Her landing was not smooth. Her parachute became tangled in a tree and the local maquis leader had to help her down.

Nancy was the middle person between London headquarters and the local maquis. The SOE sent huge numbers of weapons, equipment and money to help the French fighters. Nancy's job was to know where the planes would drop the supplies and collect it for the resistance, and also to pay the maquis fighters. She knew exactly which bridges, railway tracks and telephone wires had to be destroyed before the Allied troops could invade France. Cutting telephone wires was top priority to stop the Nazis from communicating with each other.

Nancy is most famous for taking part in a gun battle between the maquis and a large number of Nazis in June 1944. The maquis fighters were defeated and she and a small number of survivors fled the area. It was vital to warn London headquarters that the local maquis group had been destroyed. Nancy got hold of a bike to cycle 500 kilometres to the city, Châteauroux, which was where the nearest radio operator was located. She successfully alerted London headquarters with the message.

The Nazis named her the White Mouse for avoiding capture. She was on their "most wanted" list.

What happened to Nancy?

Nancy survived the war. She died in 2011 aged 99.

10 The Allies are coming!

Lise de Baissac

Born: 11th May 1905,
British Mauritius

Codename: Odile/Marguerite/
Irène/Adèle

Network name: Artist/Pimiento

Croix de Guerre
(*France*)

Knight of the Legion
of Honour (*France*)

Member of the Order
of the British Empire
(*Britain*)

Lise de Baissac's family moved to France from Mauritius
when she was a teenager in 1919. She fled France in
1940, travelling to Spain, then Portugal and arriving in
England in 1941. Lise was one of the first women to
apply for an agent role as soon as she heard the SOE was
recruiting women.

She began her training in May 1942. Most women agents became radio operators or couriers, but Lise was considered by her trainers to be talented enough to lead her own network. She was sent on two missions to France.

Along with Andrée Borrell, she was flown to France on a bomber plane. Both spies parachuted down into the French countryside as planned. They were met by agents on the ground and given their instructions.

Lise travelled to the city of Poitiers to meet with fellow agents. Her first job was to act as a courier and a contact person between the network, Scientist, the Prosper network in Paris and the Bricklayer network in Tours. All agents from the three networks could contact her for information on where to collect weapons, and for details and paperwork to help them remain undercover.

She worked alone and named her own network, Artist. She found it safer to stay away from other agents.

Lise posed as a poor widow from Paris with the cover name Madame Irène Brisse. She pretended to be an archaeologist who was searching for ancient monuments. This role allowed her to cycle all over the French countryside looking for suitable areas where the British pilots could drop supplies and also land small planes which delivered new agents.

Lise collected all the canisters which the pilots dropped and transferred them to safe houses. The canisters contained weapons, clothes and belongings of new agents who were parachuting into France.

She welcomed 13 new SOE agents and gave them their instructions. Lise also organised flights home for agents and resistance fighters whose names and faces had become known to the Nazis. They needed to flee France immediately to avoid capture.

As Lise preferred to work alone, she didn't have a radio operator who could transmit her messages to London headquarters. She had to travel to Paris and use the radio operators based there to communicate and receive her messages.

In 1943, when some of the British agents were arrested from the Prosper network, Lise fled back to London before she could be captured as well. She returned to France in 1944 with a new codename, Marguerite.

On the evening of 5th June 1944, Lise was in Paris to meet with other agents when the radio broadcaster on BBC Londres uttered the phrase "Cradle my heart with a **monotonous languor**" in French. The radio station was used to communicate secret messages to the SOE agents and maquis from London. The phrase was the signal that Churchill's Allied invasion was about to begin. All the agents and resistance fighters should be in position.

Lise immediately headed to Normandy. She needed to share all the information she had on German positions with the British officers as soon as they landed on French soil.

In the weeks after the Allied troops landed at Normandy, Lise set up landmines and tyre busters to hinder the Nazi troops.

What happened to Lise?

Lise survived the war. She died in 2004 at the age of 99.

11 The negotiator

Christine Granville

Born: 1st May 1908,
Poland

Codename: Pauline

Network name: Jockey

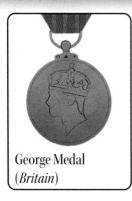

George Medal
(*Britain*)

Officer of the Order
of the British Empire
(*Britain*)

Croix de Guerre
(*France*)

The daughter of a Polish Count and his Jewish wife, Christine Granville's birth name was Krystyna Skarbek. When Germany invaded Poland, she and her husband fled to London where she took the name Christine Granville. Christine became a female agent before the SOE was set up in 1940.

She was recruited in 1939 to work as a spy and one of her
most famous achievements during the war was to smuggle
film evidence of Hitler's plan to invade the **Soviet Union**.

Near the end of the war, Christine joined the F Section and parachuted into France on 2nd March 1944.

She was famous for securing the release of two SOE agents who were being held in a German prison in 1945. With the Allied troops marching to free Europe, it was only a matter of time before Germany fell. Christine used this fact, threats and a bribe of two-million **francs** to persuade the prison commander to release her colleagues. The commander took the bribe money and set the prisoners free.

Christine was the longest serving wartime woman agent. She formally kept her cover name of Christine Granville when she became a British citizen in December 1946. She is known as one of Churchill's favourite spies.

What happened to Christine?

Christine survived the war but died a few years later in 1952.

12 Freedom

Eileen Nearne

Born: 16th March 1921, London

Codename: Rose

Network name: Wizard

Croix de Guerre
(*France*)

Member of the Order of the British Empire
(*Britain*)

Eileen Nearne was the youngest daughter of an English father and a Spanish mother. Her family moved to France in 1923. When France fell in 1940, Eileen and her older sister fled to England via Spain, Portugal, Gibraltar and Scotland.

On arrival in England, Eileen was recruited by the SOE and was flown to France on 2nd March 1944. Her mission was to help set up the Wizard network. Its only task was to supply and distribute money to help the French resistance do their work against the Nazis.

On 25th July 1944, the radio waves from Eileen's set were identified by the Nazis' tracking device while she was transmitting a message. She was immediately hunted down. She tried to hide her set from the soldiers who burst into her safe house, but it was discovered, along with her gun. She was arrested and driven to Paris to be questioned.

Eileen managed to fool the Nazi officers that she was sending messages for a businessman and she had no idea that he was British. When they demanded to know why she had done it, she replied that she was a Frenchwoman who was desperate for a job so she could have money to live. They thought she was a silly person and a waste of their time but they didn't release her. Instead, on 15th August 1944, she was sent to Ravensbrück concentration camp and then to a **forced labour camp**.

On 13th April 1945, Eileen escaped with two French women when they were taken with other prisoners into a forest. The three women hid behind trees and then ran to escape the guards. They survived for days without food.

Reaching a town, a priest hid them from Nazi soldiers in the bell tower of his church. The three women remained there until the town was liberated by the arrival of US troops. When the American soldiers stormed the church, Eileen identified herself as a British spy but they refused to believe her. Thankfully, the SOE department in London confirmed that she was one of theirs and she was allowed to return to England.

Eileen was given awards for the bravery she showed in communicating vital messages to London headquarters.

What happened to Eileen?

Eileen survived the war. She died in 2010 at the age of 89.

13 What happened to the SOE after the war?

Nazi Germany accepted defeat on 7th May 1945. The war was now over in Europe. The female SOE agents returned to England and carried on living their lives like everyone else in peacetime Britain.

In July 1945, Prime Minister Winston Churchill lost the general election. He had been an incredibly popular wartime leader, but the people wanted a different type of government now that the war was over, and Britain needed to be rebuilt.

Churchill's departure marked the end of the SOE. He had been its main founder and supporter, but other people in the government felt it had completed the task it had been set up to do. The SOE was officially abolished in January 1946.

Although the department had been shut down, the bravery, daring and courage of its agents were awarded with the highest medals after the war.

Today, the women are mentioned in history books. Some even have whole books written about them, like Noor Inayat Khan and Christine Granville. But they are not names that are easily recognised by children. The women of the SOE F Section contributed to the freedom of Great Britain and around the world. They showed incredible courage when their lives were in extreme danger. It is right that their actions were recognised with the highest bravery medals from both Britain and France.

Glossary

accountant a person whose job is to keep a record about money

Allied troops soldiers from countries working together against a common enemy

auxiliary a supportive role to people with more important roles

British embassy the office of the UK government based in other countries

British Empire in its most powerful period, Britain ruled over the countries of a quarter of the world

concentration camp prison camp where people were held in harsh conditions and many were killed

courier a person who passed on messages between different parts of a network

civilian a person who is not a member of the armed forces

descent belonging to a group of people or family

forced labour camp prisoners were forced to do hard, physical work for free

francs French money

gallantry courageous behaviour

languor feeling weak in mind or body

monotonous dull or boring

Nazi Germany official German government from 1933 to 1945, led by Adolf Hitler

networks SOE agent groups that were made up of the leader, the courier and the radio operator

Red Cross international organisation that helps people who are suffering in war

resistance fighters French people who secretly rebelled against the Nazis occupying France

sabotage destroying or obstructing something that belongs to the enemy

Soviet Union made up of countries in eastern Europe and northern Asia, and centrally ruled from Russia

troops group of soldiers in an army

Index

Spies in France

Andrée Borrel
Set up and trained local maquis groups to fight the Nazis.

Cecily Lefort
Guided RAF planes to drop canisters of supplies for Allied soldiers.

Lilian Rolfe
Transmitted information on Nazi troops' locations to London headquarters.

Denise Bloch
Multi–skilled courier and radio operator who cut crucial telephone wires to hinder the Nazis.

Pearl Witherington
A courier with a photographic memory whose own network helped sabotage Nazi activities.

Noor Inayat Khan

Radio operator who transmitted radio messages from Paris.

Nancy Wake

Trained and armed maquis with sabotage equipment to slow the Nazi response to Allied invasion.

Lise de Baissac

Worked alone to gather supply drops for sabotage activities and set up explosives on roads to slow down the Nazis.

Christine Granville

Able to get herself and others out of dangerous situations by bluffing and bribing Nazis.

Eileen Nearne

Radio operator who transmitted 105 messages to London headquarters and escaped from a prison camp.

Ideas for reading

Written by Gill Matthews
Primary Literacy Consultant

Reading objectives:
- Summarise the main ideas drawn from more than one paragraph, identifying key details that support the main ideas
- retrieve, record and present information from non-fiction

Spoken language objectives:
- articulate and justify answers, arguments and opinions
- participate in discussions, presentations, performances, role play, improvisations and debates

Curriculum links: History – a study of an aspect or theme in British history that extends pupils' chronological knowledge beyond 1066

Interest words: bravery, daring, courage

Build a context for reading
- Ask children to look at the front cover. Discuss what the title means to them and what they think the book might be about.
- Read the back-cover blurb. Explore children's knowledge and understanding of the Second World War.
- Ask what children think a spy is and what they do.
- Establish that this is an information book. Ask what organisational features it might have. Give children time to skim through the book to find the contents, glossary and index.

Understand and apply reading strategies
- Read pp2–7. Explore children's responses to the information. Discuss why the women were willing to become spies when it was so dangerous.
- Ask children to read pp8–14 and to try cracking the code on p9. Discuss the three roles that they have read about.
- Allocate Chapters 3–12 to individual children. Ask them to read their chapters and to summarise the information.
- Take feedback from the activity. Ask children what they think about the women they have read about.